TABLE OF CONTENTS

Page

ACRONYMS

BTT	Border Transition Team
CALL	Center for Army Lessons Learned
DGDP	Directorate of Graduate Degree Programs
DOD	Department of Defense
FAO	Foreign Area Officer
GDP	Graduate Degree Programs
GWOT	Global War on Terror
HTT	Human Terrain Team
SGA	Small Group Advisor

ILLUSTRATIONS

TABLES

CHAPTER 1

INTRODUCTION

> Cultural awareness will not necessarily always enable us to predict what the enemy and noncombatants will do, but it will help us better understand what motivates them, what is important to the host nation in which we serve, and how we can either elicit the support of the population or at least diminish their support and aid to the enemy.
>
> — MG Benjamin C. Freakley, CG, CJTF-76, 2006

The US Army has placed a new emphasis on cultural awareness as a key factor in combating insurgents in the operational environment. Field Manual (FM) 3-0, *Operations*, states:

> Cultural awareness helps identify points of friction within populations, helps build rapport, and reduces misunderstandings. It can improve a force's ability to accomplish its mission and provide insight into individual and group intentions. However, cultural awareness requires training before deploying to an unfamiliar operational environment and continuous updating while deployed.

Cultural awareness is a critical shortfall identified by senior Army leaders (Petraeus 2006, 51). The current training of cultural awareness at the tactical level is limited and geared toward data collection and not application. Classes on culture consist of social norms or customs and courtesies, with the end state of giving the Soldier just enough information to stay out of trouble. In order to be an enhancement to mission success, Soldiers need to develop cultural competency, not just cultural awareness to be successful in diverse cultural operations. The skill of cultural competency is often developed in combat while Soldiers are immersed in the operational environment. To truly hone skills, cultural competency must be part of the ARFORGEN training process and practiced at the collective level prior to deployment. Cultural competency needs to be developed,

1

trained, and applied, in a simulated environment replicating physical and cultural conditions prior to deployment.

The foundation for this analysis will be a definition of cultural competency at the tactical level and identification of cultural attributes a tactical unit must apply in the operational environment in order to be successful. The next step will be a proposed methodology to develop cultural competency. The third step will be a discussion of what cultural conditions to replicate in a simulated operational environment and comparison of current cultural conditions replicated by current cultural simulations. The fourth step will be the identification of shortfalls in culturally replicating the operational environment and its effect on achieving the attributes of cultural competency at the tactical level. The last step will be recommendations to overcome the shortfalls to achieve the attributes of cultural competency at the tactical level.

The importance of this research is in four areas: standardizing cultural competency training at the tactical level, identification of culturally simulated training conditions in order to achieve cultural competency, having the training capability readily available for immediate distribution and integration into training plans, and maximizing the output of the critical asset of cultural competency at the tactical level- Soldiers.

Although cultural awareness has a standard at the strategic and operational level with the National Security Strategy and FM 3-0, there is not a standard at the tactical level. A standard, as defined by Merriam Webster's dictionary is "something established by authority, custom, or general consent as a model or example" (*Merriam-Webster dictionary* 2009, s.v. "Standard"). Across the US Army, the definition, purpose and end state of cultural awareness at the tactical level is vastly different from one unit to the other. FM 3-0 states:

> Finally, complex cultural, demographic, and physical environmental factors will be present, adding to the fog of war. Such factors include humanitarian crises, ethnic and religious differences, and complex and urban terrain, which often become major centers of gravity and a haven for potential threats. The operational environment will be interconnected, dynamic, and extremely volatile. (FM 3-0 2008, 1-4)

As the US Army progresses though the modular brigade combat team concept with units attached to different headquarters across the force, the ambiguity of "what right looks like" in cultural awareness has great potential to disrupt or disintegrate the unity of effort not only at the tactical level, but at the operational and strategic level as well.

With the ambiguity of cultural awareness comes the lack of training support. The U.S. Army Training and Doctrine (TRADOC) Culture Center's mission is to "make Soldiers more aware of cultural differences" and "making the Soldiers more effective in WOT deployments" (Bonavillain 2008, 23). Although the cultural awareness training support packages (TSP) from the TRADOC Culture Center are value added to any unit, the TSP are aimed toward the individual leader and lack any collective training. By adding web-based TSPs incorporating a virtual world of interactive cultural players, groups, and conditions, the Soldier and unit would be immersed in a virtual exercise. Soldiers would have to maximize their senses making simulations a more effective training tool. The software could be easily distributed and downloaded onto networked systems at Battle Command Training Centers (BCTC) throughout the Army for immediate use.

As the TSPs are integrated into BCTCs, individual Soldiers and collective units would execute virtual missions using their warrior skills enhanced by cultural competency. FM 3-0 states cultural awareness "can improve a force's ability to accomplish its mission and provide insight into individual and group intentions" (FM 3-0 2008, 1-7). A simulation using virtual Situational Training Exercises, complete with an After Action Review capability, would improve cultural competency at the Collective level.

Using the collective concept that every Soldier is a sensor, a unit could readily increase its cultural competency. Any Soldier as part of a squad would no doubt let his immediate supervisor know that a certain person was wearing a suicide vest. The Soldier identifies the suicide vest as a symbol of danger and takes the appropriate action. What if a Soldier were trained not only to identify signs of danger but signs of cultural forms as well? As stated in FM 3-24:

> Cultural forms, such as rituals, symbols and narratives, are the medium for communicating ideologies, values, and norms that influence thought and behavior. Each culture constructs or invents its own cultural forms, through which cultural meanings are transmitted and reproduced. COIN forces can identify the belief systems of a culture by observing and analyzing its cultural forms. (FM 3-24 2006, 3-7)

A culturally simulated environment has the ability to harness the collective cultural competency of a unit and maximizing the output of the critical asset at the tactical level, the Soldier.

Cultural awareness is a key factor in military operations today, and the absence of cultural awareness in military operations is similar to solving a Rubik's cube while wearing colorblind glasses. The solution exists; however, if the patterns cannot be identified, there is no chance of solving the puzzle. Given that the US Army has

4

identified a force-wide shortfall in cultural competency, this thesis justifies the concept that a culturally simulated environment replicated within a military simulation is the most effective method to train cultural competency at the tactical level.

The next chapter will review the literature relevant to this thesis by researching cultural competency training both within the US Army and other organizations. This study will categorize the research into four distinct areas. First, culture will be defined not only by the US Army but also the business and health professions. Second, a review of US Army doctrine in reference to culture, cultural awareness, and cultural competency. Finally, what technique and procedures different professions use achieve cultural competency to complete their missions. The primary research question of this thesis is how does US Army develop cultural competency at the tactical level through military simulations? In order to explore how the US Army develops cultural competency at the tactical level through military simulations, a few questions must be answered.

1. What is the definition of cultural competency at the tactical level?

2. How does an organization train cultural competency?

3. What attributes must a unit develop at the tactical level to achieve cultural competency?

4. What are the cultural conditions of the operational environment that must be replicated in a simulated environment in order to develop cultural competency?

The importance of this research is in four areas: standardizing cultural competency training at the tactical level, identification of culturally simulated training conditions in order to achieve cultural competency, having the training capability readily available for immediate distribution and integration into training plans, and maximizing the output of the critical asset of cultural competency at the tactical level- Soldiers.

Definitions

The following terms will be used throughout the study:

Culture: An integrated system of learned behavior patterns that is characteristic of the members of any given society. Culture refers to the total way of life for a particular group of people. It includes what a group of people thinks, says, does and makes--its customs, language, material artifacts and shared systems of attitudes and feelings (Peace Corps Handbook 1997, 18).

Cultural Awareness: The ability to recognize and understand the effects of culture on people's values and behaviors (Wunderle 2006, 9).

Cultural Competence: A set of cultural behaviors and attitudes integrated in the practice methods of a system, agency or it processionals that enable them to work effectively in a cross-cultural situation (Isaacs and Benjamin 1991, 6).

Cultural Intelligence: Business term referring to the analysis of social, political, economic and other demographic information that provides an understanding of a people or nations history, institutions, psychology, beliefs and behaviors (Early and Ang 2003, 59).

Cultural Intelligence Preparation of the Battlefield (IPB): A continuous process is the expression of the mission, the actors involved, actor relationships, and events pertinent to any of the above. It is designed as an augmentation of the conventional IPB process, adding cultural qualifications to gathered intelligence, and guiding the collection process. This approach minimally perturbs the existing protocol for intelligence gathering and analysis (Davis and Fu 2004, 3).

Force Multiplier: (DOD) A capability that, when added to and employed by a combat force, significantly increases the combat potential of that force and thus enhances the probability of successful mission accomplishment.

Limitations

One limitation with this thesis is the continuous advancement of technology within military simulations. This study will compile research over a span of less than a year. The advances in computer simulations are changing rapidly and this thesis will represent only the data collected during these eight months.

CHAPTER 2

LITERATURE REVIEW

A culture is made--or destroyed--by its articulate voices.

— Ayn Rand

The recent literature articulates the knowledge of culture as an innovation way to achieve their ends. The business community, medical health, education and the Military all define, train, and utilize cultural competency is various way to achieve their end state. This chapter will explain how cultural competency is utilized by the business community, educational system, and medical healthcare field, and the current military. A discussion of cultural in military doctrine follows with a final comparison of cultural competency of the military and the medical health care field.

First, the business professions view the application of culture as an enabling variable of business performance. Most successful companies advocate trans culture competence (Hampden-Turner and Trompennaars 2000, 355) - as a unity of effort in multinational business operations. Cultural awareness, knowledge of country and populace is the base foundation for trans cultural competence but in order to apply that knowledge, teamwork and practice must be a prerequisite. Another principle of business is identifying your own culture to better work with other cultures. A common practice in the business community in to utilize a model call the cultural web. The Cultural Web identifies six interrelated elements that help to make up what Johnson and Scholes call the "paradigm"--the pattern or model--of the work environment. By analyzing the factors in each, one can begin to see the bigger picture of the organizations your culture: what systems are working, what systems are not working, and what systems need to be changed. The six elements are:

1. Stories--The past events and people talked about inside and outside the company. Who and what the company chooses to immortalize says a great deal about what it values, and perceives as great behavior.

2. Rituals and Routines--The daily behavior and actions of people that signal acceptable behavior. This determines what is expected to happen in given situations, and what is valued by management.

3. Symbols--The visual representations of the company including logos, how plush the offices are, and the formal or informal dress codes.

4. Organizational Structure--This includes both the structure defined by the organization chart, and the unwritten lines of power and influence that indicate whose contributions are most valued.

5. Control Systems--The ways that the organization is controlled. These include financial systems, quality systems, and rewards (including the way they are measured and distributed within the organization.)

6. Power Structures--The pockets of real power in the company. This may involve one or two key senior executives, a whole group of executives, or even a department. The key is that these people have the greatest amount of influence on decisions, operations, and strategic direction.

These elements are represented graphically as six semi-overlapping circles (see figure 1 below), which together influence the cultural paradigm.

In summation, the focus for training to identify and improve you own organizational culture. From that self-awareness, develop cultural intelligence, a necessity for mid managers, is an individual's ability to deal effectively with people of a different culture or background.

Second, the Education systems see cultural competence as a skill to connect with, respond to, and interact effectively with their student in an educational environment. The training of cultural competence is at the teacher or primary educator level. The emphasis is placed in the classrooms as opposed to the whole organization. R.C. Anderson, a pioneer in cultural competence in education, describes a student's organized knowledge of the world as a schema (Anderson 1984, 372). With regard to the schema, one of the educator's principal functions in teaching, particularly with literacy, is to "'bridge the gap between what the learner already knows and what he needs to know before he can successfully learn the task at hand'" (Anderson 1984, 382).

Third, the Healthcare industry believes that cultural competence is a set of cultural behaviors and attitudes integrated in the practice methods of a system, agency or it processionals that enable them to work effectively in a cross-cultural situation (guidebook on achieving cultural competence). This comprehensive approach trains all personnel to a high level of competency with a common framework for collaboration. Without cultural competence, the Health care professional cannot just do its job; the actions become detrimental in the treatment of the patient.

The current military views cultural awareness as two models. The first is data to be collected through intelligence channels and the second is a process to enable operations. With data to be collected, a series of systems are in place:

1. Cultural IPB, a continuous process, is the expression of the mission, the actors involved, actor relationships, and events pertinent to any of the above. It is designed as an augmentation of the conventional IPB process, adding cultural qualifications to gathered intelligence, and guiding the collection process (Davis and Fu 2004, 3). This approach minimally perturbs the existing protocol for intelligence gathering and analysis.

2. Cultural intelligence (Coles 2005, 1) analysis of social, political, economic and other demographic information that provides an understanding of a people or nations history, institutions, psychology, beliefs and behaviors.

3. Human Terrain (HTT): Civilian academic and military cultural expertise into the operational staff in the form of the five-man HTT. The terrain team is equipped with

computers stocked with software designed from to analysis cultural data supporting units at the Brigade level (Connable 2009, 59).

One of the primary authorities on cultural awareness as a process to enable operations is the military is LTC William D. Underlet. LTC Underlet conceptualized the capabilities as Levels in the pyramid, because military personnel with different levels and types of responsibilities (commanders versus soldiers) require different levels of cultural awareness. An explanation of the levels follows:

1. Cultural Consideration ("How and Why") is the incorporation of generic cultural concepts in common military training—knowing how and why to study culture and where to find cultural factors and expertise (Wunderle 2004, 62).

2. Cultural Knowledge (Specific Training) is exposure to the recent history of a target culture. It includes basic cultural issues such as significant groups, actors, leaders, and dynamics, as well as cultural niceties and survival language skills (Wunderle 2004, 62).

3. Cultural Understanding (Advanced Training) refers to a deeper awareness of the specific culture that allows general insight into thought processes, motivating factors, and other issues that directly support the military decision-making process (Wunderle 2004, 62).

4. Cultural Competence (Decision-making and Cultural Intelligence) is the fusion of cultural understanding with cultural intelligence that allows focused insight into military planning and decision-making for current and future military operations.[6] Cultural competence implies insight into the intentions of specific actors and groups (Wunderle 2004, 62).

In the health care industry, the Health Resources and Services Administration (HRSA), is an agency of the U.S. Department of Health and Human Services, is the principal Federal Agency charged with increasing access to health care for those who are medically underserved. HRSA's portfolio includes a range of programs or initiatives designed to increase access to care, improve quality, and safeguard the health and well-being of the Nation's most vulnerable populations (HRSA Strategic Plan 2009, 1).

When the US Army's developing of cultural competence is compare side by side by other institutions, disparities become clear.

Table 1.   Comparison of Cultural Competences

	US Army	Health Resources and Services Administration
1. In line with its published doctrine	No	Yes
2. Personnel with the most contact with the target population have the most in depth training?	No	Yes
3. No common framework	No	Yes
4. Training echelon = real world echelon	No	Yes
5. No self awareness process	No	Yes
6. Emphasize the tangibles aspects of culture	Yes	Yes
7. Emphasize the intangibles aspects of culture	Limited	Yes

Source: Created by author

In the first category is if the particular institution is in line with its current doctrine or body of teachings, the US Army is not in compliance while the cultural competence in the medical field has number policies on cultural competence being trained at the lowest level. For example, Professional societies, such as the American Medical Association and the American Nurses Association, have statements in support of, and are pursuing active agendas in, cultural competence education (Betancourt et al. 2005, 502).

The second category is the personnel in most contact with another culture have the most amount of training. Medical personnel focus cultural competency training at all levels. This allows for a holistic approach to the training of cultural competency (Martinez and Wu 2006, 3).

With current US Army doctrine, Cultural reoccurring themes are apparent in the text. These themes describe cultural competency in the operational environment in the era of persistent conflict.

Table 2. Cultural Themes in Current Doctrine

Cultural Themes in Doctrine	FM 3-0	FM 3-24	FM 3-90.6	FM 3-21-20	FM 3-21.10
Self awareness	X, X	X	X, X		X
Vital to mission success		X	X		
Damage results from lack of CA			X, X	X	X
Collective training	X, X, X	X	X, X		
Enhance operations	X, X, X				
Tangibles aspects of culture		X	X, X, X	X	X, X
Intangibles aspects of culture		X, X	X, X, X	X	

Source: Created by author

Developing cultural competency through a methodology is lacking in current literature. When dealing with ones own culture, there are models such as the cultural web but when learning another culture, most experts agree that you have to immerse yourself in that culture in order to hone your skills. For military personnel, the combat zone is too late to hone your skills. The T.E. Lawrence model suggests completing three phases in order to achieve cultural competency.

Phase 1- Orientation, this phase consists of educational background, a mentorship program, and a short term experience in the culture. The purpose of this phase is to build base knowledge of your culture (Hall 2006, 8).

Phase 2- Acculturation: the second phase, acculturation, is designed to immerse the trainees in cultural training in a non-threatening environment that brings their language skills to fluency and reinforces their earlier cultural education and training (Hall 2006, 14).

Phase 3- Application: this phase is the culmination of the previous experiences and training. This phases test you skills in a culturally diverse environment (Hall 2006, 18).

Finally when discussing cultural competency, there is one piece of literature that answers the question of what competencies tactical units must develop in order to achieve cultural competency. COL (Ret) Maxie Mcfarland in an article titled "Military Cultural Education" of March-April 2005 issue of Military Review magazine defined sixteen cultural competencies a Soldier must do in order to be cultural literate:

1. Understand that culture affects their behavior and beliefs and the behavior and beliefs of others.

2. Are aware of specific cultural beliefs, values, and sensibilities that might affect the way they and others think or behave.
3. Appreciate and accept diverse beliefs, appearances, and lifestyles.
4. Are aware that historical knowledge is constructed and, therefore, shaped by personal, political, and social forces.
5. Know the history of mainstream and nonmainstream American cultures and understand how these histories affect current society.
6. Can understand the perspective of nonmainstream groups when learning about historical events.
7. Know about major historical events of other nations and understand how such events affect behaviors, beliefs, and relationships with others.
8. Are aware of the similarities among groups of different cultural backgrounds and accept differences between them.
9. Understand the dangers of stereotyping, ethnocentrisms, and other biases and are aware of and sensitive to issues of racism and prejudice.
10. Are bilingual, multilingual, or working toward language proficiency.
11. Can communicate, interact, and work positively with individuals from other cultural groups.
12. Use technology to communicate with individuals and access resources from other cultures.
13. Are familiar with changing cultural norms of technology (such as instant messaging, virtual workspaces, E-mail, and so on), and can interact successfully in such environments.
14. Understand that cultural differences exist and need to be accounted for in the context of military operations.
15. Understand that as soldiers they are part of a widely stereotyped culture that will encounter predisposed prejudices, which will need to be overcome in cross-cultural relations.
16. Are secure and confident in their identities and capable of functioning in a way that allows others to remain secure in theirs. (McFarland 2005, 63)

If a tactical unit were to develop these sixteen competencies and leadership is able to provide strategies to deal with differences among culturally diverse people, then that unit would have the ability to be cultural competent to understand the operational environment and become a relevant factor with the population, host nation forces, and insurgent groups.

CHAPTER 3

RESEARCH DESIGN

Methodology

The framework for this analysis will research cultural competency at the tactical level by looking at the "ends, ways, and means" strategy.

First, the "ends" will define cultural competency at the tactical level and identification of cultural attributes a tactical unit must apply in the operational environment. Second, the "ways" portion focuses on a training methodology to achieve cultural competency. Third, the "means" will be a discussion of what cultural conditions are replicated in a simulated operational environment and comparison of current cultural conditions replicated by current cultural simulations. The fourth step will be the comparison of the simulations cultural conditions cross referenced by the cultural attributes a tactical unit must apply in the operational environment today. The last step will be recommendations to overcome the shortfalls to develop the attributes of cultural competency at the tactical level.

Three additional models have been introduced as a result of Cultural competency research by the author. These models are the modified version of the T. E. Lawrence model (Hall 2006, 8), the cultural cube model and cultural dynamics.

Figure 2.   Modified T. E. Lawrence Model of Learning Culture
Source: Created by author.

The T. E. Lawrence Model (Hall 2006, 8) was modified due to the nature of the tactical mission of US Army Soldiers and the ARFORGEN Cycle. The first phase of Self Evaluation was added, the process of identifying ones own culture is lacking from the original model.

The first category, cultural self evaluation, is the exploration of one's own values, norms and beliefs to identify biases. The second category, cultural education, is the process of learning the integrated pattern of human knowledge, belief, and behavior that depends upon the capacity for learning and transmitting knowledge to succeeding generations. This category also includes a comparison of one's own culture against the culture to be trained in order to identify, understand and overcome cultural differences. The third category, cultural acculturation, is the immersion into another culture. The fourth category, cultural application, is the skills to utilize cultural knowledge in another culture. These four categories will be assessed the level of current cultural training simulations at the tactical level when vetted against the cultural cube and dynamics.

Narratives (Famous + Infamous)	Formal Structure	Control
Symbols of Power	Influential Leaders	Commo
Key Players	Informal Structure	Rituals and Routines

Figure 3.   Cultural Cube

Source: Created by author.

The Cultural Cube was originally based off of the Cultural web by Johnson and Scholes for self awareness and organizational culture in the business and medical community (Jasper and Jumaa 2004, 39). The primary purpose of the cultural cube is to analyze and change the culture already embodied within your company or business practice. Although the cultural web is a quality product for a group of common professionals that already has the knowledge of the organizational hierarchal structure in mind. The Cultural cube further extended the cultural web and focuses on the people in the area of understanding for a comprehensive look at the personnel and their capabilities in not just a hierarchal structure but a horizontal structure as well. The three additional categories are formal leaders, informal leaders and key players. The need to have three separate categories of personnel in the operational area is because the counterinsurgency fight is deeply rooted in the human interaction with host nation forces, the population, and the insurgent forces. Knowing how to build relationships or break ties to other relationships is essential to becoming relevant in the operational environment. The first step to the process is knowing who to build relationships with or at least identifying that you cannot build a successful relationship but who to marginalize in their own relationship building. One must perform detailed analysis to identify formal leaders, informal leaders, and key players in the population. The definition of a formal leader is an individual who have been given title and authority to influence others to achieve established organizational goals and objectives. This person is generally measured and incentivized by their ability to motivate the team to accomplish these goals. Success of the formal leader is linked directly to performance of the team. If the team does well, the leader is considered a success.

The second additional category is Informal leaders. An informal leader is an individual, without formal title or authority, who is perceived by the group as an individual worthy of being followed. This may be because of subject matter expertise, longevity with the group, or prior successes recognized by the group. Informal leaders are critical to the success of the team and may wield more power and influence than the formal leader.

There are key differences between formal and informal leaders. First, the informal leaders are not accountable to the same group goals and metrics assigned to the formal leader. Second, an informal leader's influence can extend to areas outside of the groups goals. Third, informal leaders demonstrate leadership traits that are recognized by the

20

group such as motivation, mentorship, and inspiration. Formal leaders may or may not have these characteristics. Finally, an informal leader has garnered the trust and respect of the group. For the Formal Leader, this may be something that often has to be earned and tested time and time again with major decisions.

The cultural cube is a model that identifies nine interrelated elements that help to make up the intangibles of a culture. By analyzing the factors in each, one can begin to see the interconnectivity of the culture:

Narratives--The past events and people talked about inside and outside the culture. Who and what the people choose to immortalize says a great deal about what it values, and perceives as great behavior.

Formal Structure--Duties, powers and rights that correspond to positions in that culture.

Informal Structures--Influence of social networks through beliefs and customs in that culture

Rituals and Routines--The daily behavior and actions of people that signal acceptable behavior. This determines what is expected to happen in given situations, and what is valued in the culture.

Symbols of power--The visual representations of the important concepts or objects that the valued by the people.

Influential Leaders--Leaders whose actions and opinions strongly influence the course of events in the culture.

Communication--mediums in which cultures pass information.

Key players--the most important positions in a formal structure to accomplish tasks (this may or may not be one of the leaders).

Control Systems--The ways that the people are controlled. These include financial systems, quality systems, and rewards (including the way they are measured and distributed within the culture.)

Although the military currently uses PMESII (political, military, economic, social, information and infrastructure) to define the operational environment, that system focuses on the tangible aspects of an environment. Many of the tangible aspects of a society are easily be identified by Intelligence, Surveillance, and Reconnaissance, and then targeted with precision weaponry. For example, when dealing with another nation's military, you can identify regular armed forces and military elite forces during campaign planning. However, when dealing with the intangible aspects of a society, such as symbols of power or informal structure, the utility of the PMESII construct is significantly diminished (Arnold 2006, 3). The cultural cube is better suited because it focuses on the intangible aspects of a culture rather than the tangible aspects.

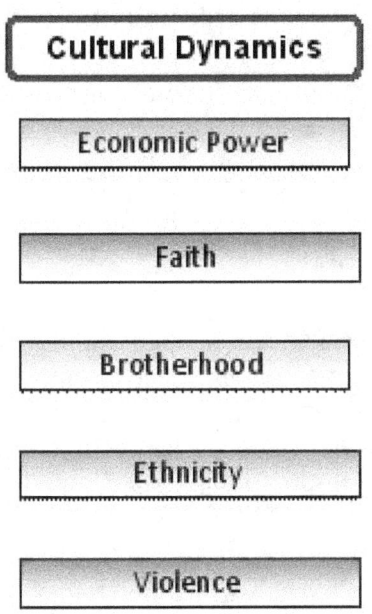

Figure 4.   Cultural Dynamics

Source: Created by author.

The cultural dynamics is a model to compare two or more groups in the same culture or different cultures and how they interact with each others.

Economic power: the condition of having sufficient productive resources at command that give the capacity to make and enforce economic decisions, such as allocation of resources and apportioning of goods and services.

Faith: belief in the doctrines or teachings of religion.

Brotherhood: an association for a particular purpose.

Ethnicity: Identity with or membership in a particular racial, national, or cultural group and observance of that group's customs, beliefs, and language.

Violence: physical force used to inflict injury or damage

CHAPTER 4

ANALYSIS

The Ends, Ways, and Means of Cultural Competency

Another aspect of readiness for expeditionary operations is awareness of other cultures and languages. We are expanding our investments in training and education programs to enhance language training and cultural orientation in service schools. We are also placing greater emphasis in these areas at our Combat Training Centers, evidenced in both design of training rotations and scenarios for role players. Leaders must continue to stress cultural awareness during pre-deployment training, leader development, and in other initiatives.

— GEN Peter J. Schoomaker, CSA

Analysis of the "Ends"

Cultural competency and understanding the culture in your operational environment is a key factor to working within the operational environment today. Admiral (retired) Arthur Cebrowski, Director of Transformation, Office of the Secretary of Defense (OSD) states, "Even today, the knowledge of one's enemy and his culture and society may be more important than knowledge of his order of battle." Yet, in current literature, there is not one consensus as to what is the correct definition of culture.

The official definition of culture used by DOD and the North Atlantic Treaty Organization (NATO) can be found in Joint Publication (JP 1-02), Department of Defense Dictionary of Military and Associated Terms. Culture is defined as "a feature of the terrain that has been constructed by man. Included are such items as roads, building, and canals, boundary lines and in a broad sense, all names and legends on a map." This definition is clearly illustrates the lack of human intangibles found with a population's culture. By focusing on the material aspects of culture, one would never be able to learn about the intangibles of culture to become relevant in the operational environment.

24

When used in context with intangible aspects, Joint Doctrine states: "Much of the information and guidance provided for joint operations is applicable to multinational operations; however, differences in allied doctrine, organization, weapons and equipment, terminology, culture , religion, and language must be taken into account." This definition indicates that culture is separate instance of religion and language when, in fact, both language and religion are critical components of culture. Without having a precise definition of culture leads to misunderstandings of the concept.

When defining culture, key aspects of the tangible as well as the intangible must be including into the definition for a holistic approach to understanding people and their way of life. Culture is defined by this thesis as "an integrated system of learned behavior patterns that is characteristic of the members of any given society. Culture refers to the total way of life for a particular group of people. It includes what a group of people thinks, says, does and makes--its customs, language, material artifacts and shared systems of attitudes and feelings" (Peace Corps Handbook 1997, 18).

In addition to not having a complete definition for culture, there is no standardized definition for cultural competency. There are many innuendos for cultural competency in doctrine such as cultural savvy, cultural understanding, or cultural awareness but these innuendos are the part of cultural competency and never defined as a whole. The lack of common operational picture for what cultural competency look like again leads to confusion and hampers unity of effort. Cultural competency is defined by this thesis as a "set of cultural behaviors and attitudes integrated in the practice methods of a system, agency or its professionals that enable them to work effectively in a cross-cultural situation" (Cross, Cultural Competence in Healthcare, 5).

Although culture and cultural competency are not clearly defined in doctrine, there are common themes in doctrine related to culture and cultural competency. When looking at the narratives given in FM 3-0, FM 3-24, FM 3-90.6, FM 3-21.20, and FM 3-21.10, there are six overall cultural themes that permeate through the doctrine.

1. Cultural awareness is a process of self awareness

2. Cultural understanding is vital to mission success.

3. Lack of cultural understanding is damaging to the unit and mission.

4. Cultural awareness should be trained at the collective level.

5. Cultural understanding enhances effects operations.

6. Cultural awareness is both the tangibles and intangible.

The first cultural theme is that cultural awareness is a process of self-awareness. In order to learn another culture, one must first know one's own culture. This is a common practice in many models such as the cultural web. FM 3-24 states that American ideas of what is normal or rational are not universal. FM 3-90.6 states that are differences in what indigenous populations and coalitional partners value. The inference application is that one must know his own culture to identify any differences in another culture. Once the differences are identified, then the next logical step is to marginalize or neutral the biases to foster unity of effort.

The second cultural theme is cultural understanding is vital to mission success. FM 3-24 states that cultural knowledge is essential when developing host nation forces or establishing rapport with the local population. FM 3-90.6 states that key beliefs, values behaviors and norms are imperative to mission success. Any ground forces operating within a culture different from their own, will have to learn about that culture in order to effectively work within that culture.

The third cultural theme is a lack of cultural understanding is damaging to the unit and mission. This theme is based on comments in FM 3-21-20 which states, Ethnocentrism and cultural arrogance can damage relationships with other forces, NGOs, or indigenous populations. FM 3-90.6 discusses how actions or speech that might insult or offend the members of certain cultures when one is does not have cultural understanding. The end result is a unit that is not effective in working with other cultures either by arrogance or naivety of their traditions beliefs or values systems.

The fourth cultural theme is that cultural competence should be trained at the collective level. FM 3-0 states how cultural understanding improves the forces ability to accomplish its mission. FM 3-21.10 states that defining other influential organizations or groups of influence allows for effective information collection and intelligence gathering. With intelligence gathering commonly using the techniques of every Soldier is a senor or every and every patrol giving a patrol debrief, one can imply that indentifies certain aspect of a indigenous populations culture needs to be trained at the collective level since that is the standard operating procedures in combat.

The fifth cultural theme is that knowledge of a culture enhances operations. FM 3-0 states that units need to leverage local culture to enhance the effectiveness of their operations. FM 3-24 states Intimate cultural familiarity and knowledge of insurgent myths, narratives and culture are a prerequisite to accomplishing the mission

The last cultural theme is that culture is both tangibles and intangibles of a population and the intangibles of a population. FM 3-24 states Social structure can be

27

thought of as a skeleton, and culture is like the muscle on the bones. The two are mutually dependent and reinforcing, and a change in one results in a change in the other. If one just understands what one can see when working with or against local forces, then one will not be completely successful in the operational environment.

As with any military operation, one has to define the end state in order to drive the unity of effort towards mission accomplishment. Now that culture and cultural competency are standardized and defined, doctrine has given overarching cultural guidance; one has to define the end state of cultural competency at the tactical level. The competencies a tactical unit should have in order to develop cultural competency define the end state.

Taking the definition of culture and competence, and understanding the cultural themes in doctrine that describe culture in the operational environment, to answer the question of what competencies tactical units develop in order to achieve cultural competency, COL (Ret) Maxie Mcfarland in an article titled "Military Cultural Education" of March-April 2005 issue of *Military Review* defined sixteen cultural competencies a Soldier must do in order to be cultural literate:

> 1. Understand that culture affects their behavior and beliefs and the behavior and beliefs of others.
> 2. Are aware of specific cultural beliefs, values, and sensibilities that might affect the way they and others think or behave.
> 3. Appreciate and accept diverse beliefs, appearances, and lifestyles.
> 4. Are aware that historical knowledge is constructed and, therefore, shaped by personal, political, and social forces.
> 5. Know the history of mainstream and nonmainstream American cultures and understand how these histories affect current society.
> 6. Can understand the perspective of nonmainstream groups when learning about historical events.
> 7. Know about major historical events of other nations and understand how such events affect behaviors, beliefs, and relationships with others.

28

8. Are aware of the similarities among groups of different cultural backgrounds and accept differences between them.

9. Understand the dangers of stereotyping, ethnocentrisms, and other biases and are aware of and sensitive to issues of racism and prejudice.

10. Are bilingual, multilingual, or working toward language proficiency.

11. Can communicate, interact, and work positively with individuals from other cultural groups.

12. Use technology to communicate with individuals and access resources from other cultures.

13. Are familiar with changing cultural norms of technology (such as instant messaging, virtual workspaces, E-mail, and so on), and can interact successfully in such environments.

14. Understand that cultural differences exist and need to be accounted for in the context of military operations.

15. Understand that as soldiers they are part of a widely stereotyped culture that will encounter predisposed prejudices, which will need to be overcome in cross-cultural relations.

16. Are secure and confident in their identities and capable of functioning in a way that allows others to remain secure in theirs. (McFarland 2005, 63)

If a tactical unit were to develop these sixteen competencies in combination with leadership and a comprehensive strategy, that unit would have the ability to be cultural competent to understand the operational environment and become a relevant factor with the population, host nation forces, and insurgent groups.

Defining the "Ways"

What are the training "ways" to develop the sixteen cultural competencies in the operational environment? We must look at the training of culture in order to achieve the training approach.

The Army has many programs that are designed to build cultural competency, including multinational and partnership training exercise programs and officer-exchange programs. These programs are constructive, but, unfortunately, are based on educating the foreign Soldiers on U.S. cultural norms and operations rather than the opposite (McFarland 2005, 6).

Unit cultural pre-deployment programs often teach the regional specific cultural norms of the theater but are often too broad in scope to be useful and focus on the "dos and do not's" necessary to avoid offending a person of that culture.

Based on the modified T. E. Lawrence model (Hall 2006), a unit must complete four phases to achieve cultural competence. First, self evaluation of the units own culture and cultural biases. Second, the unit must execute cultural education on the area of operations. Third, the unit must be immersed in the culture in order to practice the skill. Last, the unit must be able to apply the culture skills in the environment.

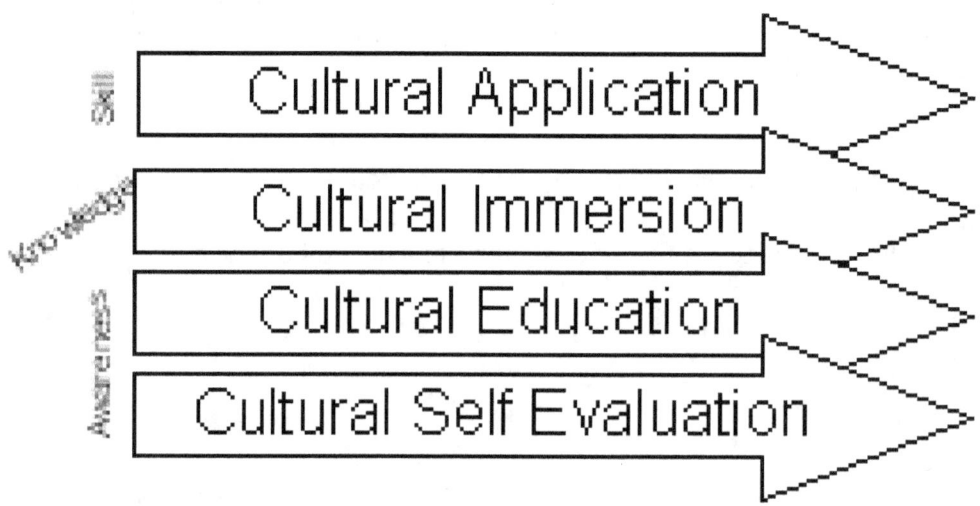

Figure 5.   Modified T. E. Lawrence Model of Learning Culture
Source: Created by author.

According to B. M. Rodriquez, an advocate of cross-cultural competency in education, cultural self-awareness is a bridge to other cultures. The first step in that bridge is an awareness of one's own heritage, encounters and experiences. This self-awareness will facilitate one's capacity to:

- Explore, understand, acknowledge, and value our cultural and social background regarding 'race,' ethnicity, social class, gender, regionalism, sexual orientation, exceptionality, age, religion/spirituality, language, and dialect.
- Increase our awareness and insight into our own learning processes, strengths, weaknesses, successes, failures, biases, values, goals, and emotions.
- Experience our own cultures in relation to others as they are illuminated during cross-cultural interactions.
- Understand and respond to areas of conflict and tension when we encounter individuals from unfamiliar cultures or experiences, and learn to be more comfortable with being uncomfortable.
- Explore and appreciate thought processes that occur across cultures but may also take on different shapes and meanings for different cultural groups and for individual group members.
- Understand and respect more deeply the cultural values and beliefs of those with whom we come in contact. (Rodriquez 1999, 14)

Self evaluation should be executed in two parts. The first part is an exercise in self-awareness of the individual Soldier. By critically thinking about their experiences and through the categories of the cultural cube, Soldiers can become awareness of their own beliefs and biases. Next, as a group, the unit can come to a consensus as to a combined unit culture. This will identify cultural beliefs and cultural biases as a group and help facilitate their cross-cultural interaction in the area of operations. A way to help a Soldier or unit with self- awareness is to utilize the cultural cube outlined in this thesis as a model for introspection. The categorized can be modified but will at least give a base foundation for beliefs and norms.

After learning of one's own culture and unit culture, the unit must educate itself on the specifics of the culture or cultures in their area of operations. Utilizing the cultural cube as a framework, Soldiers must understand the intangible aspects of the group's way of life. Soldiers must then understand how groups interact with the cultural dynamics for that region. The cultural dynamics can change from what is listed below but the main purpose is to capture the important aspects of what motivates a culture.

Narratives (Famous + Infamous)	Formal Structure	Control
Symbols of Power	Influential Leaders	Commo
Key Players	Informal Structure	Rituals and Routines

Figure 6.　Cultural Cube

Source: Created by author.

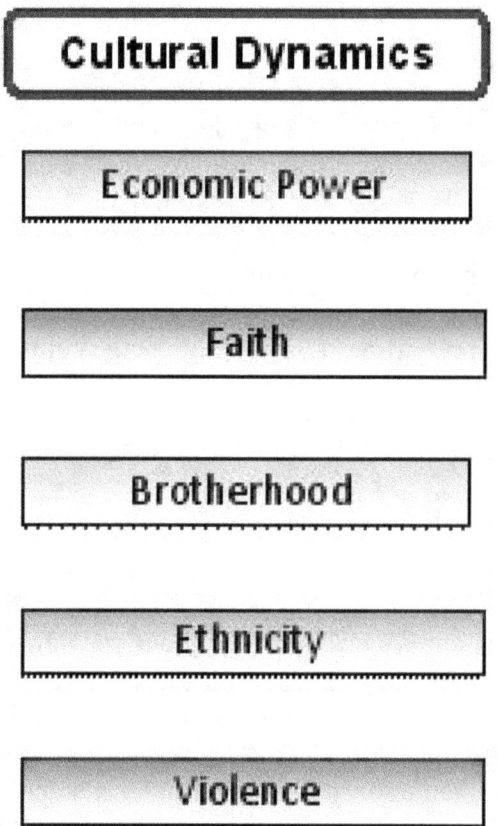

Figure 7.　Cultural Dynamics

Source: Created by author.

Once a unit has completed a cultural self evaluation and the unit has been educated on the culture in their area of operations, the next step is to be immersed in that culture. This phase need to be hands on and challenging in order to be realistic. This must also be a non-threatening environment that reinforces a unit's earlier cultural training. This could be in the form of simulation such as ELECT BiLAT or Tactical Iraqi. The goal of this phase is to provide an avenue for some direct application of the newly acquired cultural education and turn said education into knowledge.

Once unit gains knowledge of an area, the next step is the cultural application phase where all of the prior training is put to the test. This could be in a simulation with a challenging thinking enemy, at any one of the combat training centers or the real world deployment. The difference between cultural immersion and cultural application is that the application phase has direct consequences for their actions. Cultural immersion is putting someone in that culture to absorb the intangible aspects of that culture. Cultural application is when you have generally absorbed the intangible aspects of that culture and are not ready to start making decisions and taking actions to become relevant in the operational environment.

Defining the "Means"

The "means" to develop cultural competency is physically and culturally simulate an environment for the interaction and feedback of the training audience. The physical representation of an operational environment is done very well through simulations such as VBS 2 or the CTCs with their training villages and role-players. In most simulations, the terrain and infrastructure resembles village and cities in Iraq.

When it comes to modeling culture in order to have an environment for cultural competency, the design becomes a bit difficult. There are four reasons why it is so difficult. First, there is not a standardized framework to properly articulate the culture of a population such as the cultural cube and cultural dynamics. This lack of framework does not allow for a dialogue between persons and cannot form a common operational picture for the group. Second, programmers can build any simulation but they need to know what culture factors to program into the simulation. There is not a standardized army framework cultural to discuss and analyze the intangibles of culture. With that lack of a cultural framework such as a cultural cube or cultural dynamics, it is very hard to describe the intangibles of what needs to be in a simulation. Third, once the culture factors are programmed into the simulation, those culture factors must be flexible to change. Based on the interaction with the training audience, the simulation must correctly react either positively or negatively, to truly culturally replicate the environment. Last, how do we know the cultural intangibles we programmed are working correctly? When terrain is replicated, it is simple to verify accuracy, it either looks like the terrain on the ground or it does not. With cultural intangibles, how to we know the character in the simulations is acting the right way? What are the metrics for accuracy? This ambiguity also adds to the problem of developing cultural competency.

The final portion of the analysis is to analyze the current training simulations that declare cultural training and cross reference that training against the cultural themes in doctrine in order to evaluate the simulation.

Table 3.   Simulations with Limited Cultural Emphasis

Simulations	Tactical Iraqi	Elect BILAT	VBS 2
Primary purpose	Language Trainer	Negotiations Trainer	Tactical training
Declared cultural aspect	Cultural Awareness Trainer	Cultural Sensitivity Trainer	Cultural Awareness Trainer

Source: Created by author.

There are currently three simulations with limited cultural interaction. The first simulation is Tactical Iraqi, the second simulation is Elect BILAT, and the third simulation is VBS 2.

Tactical Iraqi is a simulation that focuses on honing language skills. Tactical Iraqi also teaches some cultural knowledge, such as non-verbal gestures, etiquette, and norms of politeness. This cultural knowledge is specific to language communication and can help the trainee effectively get his meaning across to someone of Iraqi culture without offending the person. I found tactical Iraqi to be an interactive video game from the first person perspective that simulates conversations with virtual people who react to the proper speech and body language of my avatar. This feedback is provided in observable trust meter. The trust meter represents how much the virtual person I am having a virtual conversation with trusts me enough to give me truthful information. If the game character does not trust the game user based on offense speech or gestures, the game character will give faulty information or no information at all.

When compared against the cultural themes in doctrines some gaps become apparent.

Table 4. Tactical Iraqi	
Cultural themes in Doctrine	Application in Simulation
1. Cultural awareness is a process of self awareness	Not applied
2. Cultural understanding is vital to mission success	Yes
3. Lack of cultural understanding is damaging to the unit and mission	Limited
4. Cultural awareness should be trained at the collective level.	Not applied
5. Cultural understanding enhances operations.	Limited
6. Cultural awareness is both the tangibles and intangibles	Very Limited

Source: Created by author.

When cross referenced against the first theme in doctrine of self awareness, the first training gap is the lack of self awareness training. Without having the self awareness training, one cannot indentify and prepare for individual cultural biases. It can be argued that Tactical Iraqi was not built for that learning objective. If that is the case than, there should be a pre-requisite prior to executing Tactical Iraqi that a model of self awareness should be completed in order to be in compliance with doctrine.

Tactical Iraqi does appreciate the second theme is doctrine that cultural understanding is vital to mission success. Without the proper combination of Arabic phases and corresponding gestures, you will not be able to accomplish your mission. This simple learning technique relays the message that effective communication needs cultural understanding.

The third theme is hard to evaluate by the simple fact that tactical Iraqi is a single layer game. A lack of understanding is damaging to the unit and mission is somewhat inferred since a Soldier does not operate alone in the operational environment alone the lack of other personnel of your unit with whom to interact by either multiplier or artificial intelligence only stifles this cultural theme. One does understand that by not receiving information or observing your trust meter progressively measuring lower due to offending people that a lack of cultural understanding is damaging to the mission.

The fourth theme of cultural awareness should be trained at the collective level is again hampered by the fact that Tactical Iraqi is a single person game. The result is Tactical Iraqi, in a current configuration as a single player game, cannot train at the collective level.

The fifth theme of cultural awareness enhances operations is inferred at the individual level of this simulation but would be better maximized as a multiplayer game. The term military operations inferred the actions are executed collectively as a unit. With this inference in mind, Tactical Iraqi is very limited in its approach.

The last cultural theme is that culture is articulated as both the tangibles and intangibles of culture. Tactical Iraqi does a very good job of immersing a person in the tangibles of culture, complete with landscape, language and gestures. Tactical Iraqi is very limited when it comes to the intangibles of culture.

When referring to the intangibles of a culture, I will use the cultural cube as a model to see the effectiveness of replicating a cultural environment.

Table 5.	Tactical Iraqi
Cultural Cube	Application in Simulation
1. Narratives	Not applied to the population
2. Formal Structure	Limited
3. Informal Structures	Not applied
4. Rituals and Routines	Not applied to the population
5. Symbols of power	Not applied
6. Influential Leaders	Not applied to the population
7. Communication	Spoken Language only
8. Key Players	Not applied to the population
9. Control Systems	Not applied

Source: Created by author.

The first category within the cultural cube is narratives. There are narratives within Tactical Iraqi but they are more stories to lead you to the next person and not who the particular group of people chooses to immortalize as being famous or infamous. From these stories, you could not make a formal assessment as to whom or what is being immortalized and how the group values the characteristics or actions of that group.

Formal Structure is replicated to a limited manner in this simulation, this replication is just enough to know the Sheik is the leader of a people or the mayor is the head of the town. It does not have the specifics as to their powers or rights as the Sheik, Mayor, and others. This lack of depth does not allow for full analysis of their capabilities and influence on the population. Without knowing which leaders are influential on the population, one cannot maximize unity of effort with host nation forces, government leaders, and others.

Informal Structures are replicated in this simulation but only through customs and not beliefs. By only learning the customs in this environment, one only has half the story. The true meaning of an informal structure is motivated by the beliefs in the environment. Who is intimidating in the town and why? What actions step over the line of offending and cause a negative action by a person with devious intent within the group? The lack of this category leaves an absence of realism.

The rituals and routines within Tactical Iraqi are limited to the interaction between persons. This is helpful as a one individual but the lack of identification of behaviors and actions of groups of people that signal acceptable behavior does not give the player the analytical skills to identify the commonalities and difference in groups of personnel in his operational environment.

Symbols of power, the visual representations of the important concepts or objects that the valued by the group or groups, is not maximized within this simulations. The lack of symbols of power identified by different groups does not develop the analytical skills to identify the commonalities and differences in the various groups within the area of operations.

Influential Leaders are replicated within Tactical Iraqi but it is leaders who are pro-coalition intentions and not leaders who have anti-coalition intentions.

With tactical Iraqi being a language familiarly tool, communication through spoken language is well communicated. What is lacking is the realism of how and frequency their communication is best influenced on the population such as town hall meeting or a radio show.

Key players are important positions in a formal structure to accomplish tasks. Key player may or may not be the leaders. This is replicated in the simulation but not enough to give the user a point of leverage to pursue a certain agenda. Most key players, who are not leaders, can point you in the right direction to the particular leader who will help you with a task but cannot assist in achieving a task.

Control Systems are replicated to a small degree within the simulation. If is difficult to identify the specific ways people are control other than law and certain customs. The intangible ways people are controlled such as intimidation or bribes are not replicated or measure to any degree as a factor in the game play.

Overall the cultural cube is not replicated to any significance depth of substance and what little is replicated cannot be measured multiple perspectives.

As a specific language trainer, Tactical Iraqi is an effective method to develop the cognitive skills of communication in a cross cultural environment. As a cultural awareness trainer, Tactical Iraqi falls short with its lack of cultural cube attributes and should be categorized as a limited cultural educational tool.

ELECT BiLAT is the next simulation for analysis. ELECT BiLAT is an acronym that stands for Enhanced Learning Environment with Creative Technologies Bilateral negotiations.

Already in use by tactical units for training, ELECT BiLAT is a simulation is designed to put emphasis on cultural sensitivity in negotiation skills while immersed in a cross cultural environment.

When cross referenced against the cultural themes in doctrine, ELECT BiLAT has depth in certain area to allow for a release replication of certain tangibles and intangibles of a culture but still is limited in its application in the cultural themes.

Table 6. ELECT BiLAT	
Cultural themes in Doctrine	Application in Simulation
1. Cultural awareness is a process of self awareness	Not applied
2. Cultural understanding is vital to mission success	Yes
3. Lack of cultural understanding is damaging to the unit and mission	Yes
4. Cultural awareness should be trained at the collective level.	Not applied
5. Cultural understanding enhances operations.	Limited
6. Cultural awareness is both the tangibles and intangibles	Limited

Source: Created by author.

ELECT BiLAT does not bring the user through a process of self awareness. By negating this process, the issue of cultural bias is still within the realm of the simulation. The definition of cultural sensitivity is a person knowing that cultural differences as well as similarities exist, without assigning values, better or worse, right or wrong, to those cultural differences (Stafford et al. 1997, 23). Based on that definition, an implied subtask to discover what the cultural differences are through the process of self awareness. Once identified through the process of self-awareness, one must marginalizing potential friction points of two cultures in order to gain cultural sensitivity.

The next cultural theme of cultural understanding being vital to mission success is apparent in the simulation. Fostering positive conditions for negotiations and identifying windows of opportunity, per FM 3-24, are keys for leveraging your points during you negotiations. Without cultural understand, the simulation will not allow for effective negations. ELECT BiLAT does a very good job of conveying this theme in the simulation.

Lack of cultural understanding is damaging to the unit or mission is the next theme in the simulation. ELECT BiLAT does another very good job of conveying this message. A negotiations plan without cultural information as an important part of that plan will do poorly in the simulation. In order to achieve this cultural information, there as a series of background information that must be investigated in order to be successful. Although based on a single person and not a group of people, this technique displays the importance of finding out narratives or beliefs of a certain person and could be applied to a group.

The theme of cultural awareness should be applied at the collective level is not applicable since ELECT BiLAT, in its current configuration, is a single player game.

In the fifth theme of cultural awareness enhances operations is inferred at the individual level of this simulation but would be better maximized as a multiplayer game. As with the previous simulation of Tactical Iraqi, the term military operations inferred the actions are executed collectively as a unit. With this inference in mind, ELECT BiLAT is also very limited in its approach.

In reference to the sixth theme of cultural awareness is the ability to understand both the tangibles and intangibles of a culture, ELECT BiLAT is more robust than

42

Tactical Iraqi but still limited in its scope. ELECT BiLAT gives the user a solid application of the tangibles through norms and customs but still is still limited to a single player forum. Although some intangibles of culture are determined such as informal structure of corruption and rituals and routines of the population as the marketplace is a main point in the story. These intangibles are still in name only and do not give the user the ability to actually see the rituals and routine, just read the text on the report. This lack of realism prevents ELECT BiLAT from maximizing the potential to understand the intangibles of culture.

Table 7. ELECT BiLAT	
Cultural Cube	Application in Simulation
1. Narratives	Not applied to the population
2. Formal Structure	Limited
3. Informal Structures	Limited
4. Rituals and Routines	Limited
5. Symbols of power	Not applied to the population
6. Influential Leaders	Not applied to the population
7. Communication	Spoken Language and text
8. Key Players	Not applied to the population
9. Control Systems	Not applied to the population

Source: Created by author.

Narratives are the first category of the cultural cube and are not applied to the population as a whole in this simulation. Although stories are used to convey messages, the stories are straightforward and geared about an individual. The learning point of what a populations values through their stories, both good and bad, is lost by speaking about an individual.

The formal and informal structures of the society is described in some detail within ELECT BiLAT but not experienced in this immerse environment. Then lack of Soldiers personally dealing with and verifying the formal and informal structure does not allow for a common operational picture of all the structures with in a society. By not observing the structures leads to a lack the metrics to verify which structure is better to use in a certain situation.

Rituals and routines are also described by either text or conversation but lack the observation to verity or test the validity of the reports. By not being able to observe and the population, one cannot fully develop the cognitive skill to identify all the rituals and routines of the target groups.

The visual representations of the important concepts or objects that the valued by the group or groups, Symbols of power, are not maximized within this simulations. Certain symbols are discussed within the conversation, but not visually observed within the context of group's actions. This lack of group interaction leaders to a lack of metrics to measure the affect of a symbol of power on a group action in order to assess how this symbol can be used or not used in future situations.

Influential leaders are portrayed in the one on one negotiation. Outside the negotiation, the affect on the population of the society by the influential leaders are not seen. Without this certain game play, a leader cannot assess who is more influential on the population or through what actions the leader achieves his influence.

The definition of a key player is an important position in a formal structure to accomplish tasks that may or may not be a leader. The aspect of the cultural cube is replicate through only a leader in this category and not people who are not key players. This replicates the formal structure but has a gap for someone who is not a leader still necessary to accomplish the task in a formal structure.

Control systems are simulated in ELECT BiLAT through the conversation with the virtual local actor or in text from reports. Without having the game play to see the control systems on the population, the game user cannot see the affects of control on the population. This lack of observable information forces the game user to take at face value any control systems discussed in the conversation but missies any other non-formal control systems (such as corruption or intimidation) hat are also in the operational environment.

Overall, ELECT BiLAT is a robust, negotiator tool that used cultural knowledge in an effective manner in a simulated office. ELECT BiLAT can assist with planning with cultural knowledge but the lack of actions at the individual or unit level leave a gap in the application of cultural knowledge on a population in a simulated operational environment.

The third simulation for analysis is Virtual Battlespace 2 (VBS2). Virtual Battle space 2 (VBS 2) "is a fully interactive, three-dimensional training system providing a premium synthetic environment suitable for a wide range of military (or similar) training and experimentation purposes," (definition from website). VBS2's primary purpose is a tactical trainer. Bohemia Interactive Australia, the parent company of the simulation, states on their website that VBS2 offers both virtual and constructive interfaces onto high-fidelity worlds of unparalleled realism. This simulation has the most potential to teach culture out of the three discussed but is limited by the person creating the scripting of the scenario.

The current version of VBS 2 has limited aspects of culture consisting of ten cultural observable gestures in the simulation. These cultural observably gestures are not enough information to assess a full picture in the culture cube or understand the cultural dynamics of a group of people. VBS 2 does have the potential to replicate the categories of the cultural cube and be in compliance with the cultural themes in doctrine based on capabilities of the simulation.

Two capabilities of VBS which allow for cultural training potential is dynamic scripting and scenario editing.

Dynamic scripting is the ability to convey a detailed storyline or thread within a scenario in order to achieve specific training objectives. Dynamic scripting also allows for adjustments in the storyline or thread while the scenario is executing. This process allows for realistic feedback based on the actions of the game player or players and not on a scenario already preconceived regardless of game players input.

Scenario design is the changing or adjusting of the scenario. This editing can be physical such as terrain and weather, or intangible such as the mood of a population. Scenario edition can also be executed during the training exercise and adjusted as necessary, making for a realistic situation.

As VBS2 is cross referenced against the cultural themes in doctrine, there is possible application of the themes in the simulation that is based on a cultural rich training scenario.

Table 8. VBS 2	
Cultural themes in Doctrine	Application in Simulation
1. Cultural awareness is a process of self awareness	Potential based on scenario
2. Cultural understanding is vital to mission success	Potential based on scenario
3. Lack of cultural understanding is damaging to the unit and mission	Potential based on scenario
4. Cultural awareness should be trained at the collective level.	Potential based on scenario
5. Cultural understanding enhances operations.	Potential based on scenario
6. Cultural awareness is both the tangibles and intangibles	Potential based on scenario

Source: Created by author.

With VBS2 already equipped as a multiplayer experience, the process of self awareness could be a simple dialogue between players crafted with the right agenda. In this virtual meeting, Soldier could reflect upon their personal experiences to identify cultural bias. Soldiers could then discuss the group dynamics and come to a consensus of the group culture. This virtual meeting could easily be scripted into the scenario to accomplish this task and have the right foundation of self actualization before operating in a culture not their own.

The second theme of cultural understanding is vital to mission success can be replicated a number of ways into a mission oriented scenario. A potential scenario is for a squad or platoon is to identity someone in the town perpetrating anti-government rhetoric within the town. The Mayor and other formal leaders have already been ruled out. The unit must identify the informal leaders of the population based on the effect of the people within the village. The Soldiers can collectively look and listen while on patrol and analyze at their virtual CP to decide who of the indigenous population is the most influential without a formal position of power. When a group of indigenous persons have been identified as potential informal leaders by the multiple perspectives from the group, Soldiers can then put in rank order who is the most influential and who is the least influential. The next step would be to discuss what methods they use to be influential. Fear, intimidation, coercion, and persuasion can all be replicated in the simulation with personnel playing virtual avatars or computer generated avatars with specific limited scripts. This information will potential lead to a collective mission with specific intelligence gathering rewards to convey the message that cultural understanding is vital to mission success.

The same scenario that conveyed mission successes can also be dynamically scripted to convey the third cultural theme, the lack of cultural awareness can be damaging to the unit and mission. The proper scenario can foster the conditions in the operational environment of rights and rituals, symbols of power, and other cultural characteristics. If Soldiers cannot collectively look and listen for those characteristics, then the scripting thread cannot be obtained and the mission will not be achieved.

The use of multiplayer in VBS2 could truly replicate the Soldiers of that unit and fulfills the forth cultural theme of collective training. The number of multiplayer participants is dependent on networking and other technical features but the average VBS2 training package has approximately thirty players.

VBS2's robust scripting practices allow for varying degrees of success in operations. A potential scenario for the fifth cultural theme of cultural understanding enhances operations is the identification of certain symbols of power within a population such as a mark of a political party that has anti-government forces ties. This subtle innuendo in the script has potential to lead the training audience to a more rewarding mission such a high value target (HVT).

The terrain and modeling in VBS2 is very vigorous and is continuously being improved. The terrain in VBS2 allows for geo-specific replication given enough information on the land. The modeling feature in the simulation is also robust and has for accurate 3D modeling of detailed replications of weapons and infrastructure. This allows for the VBS2 editor to create as specific environment to detail the tangibles of culture.

The ability to allow for avatars by cultural experts has potential to expose the intangibles of cultural as well based the focus scripting.

The specifics of the cultural cube characteristics modeled within VBS2 are based on the scripting process.

Table 9. VBS2	
Cultural Cube	Application in Simulation
1. Narratives	Potential based on scenario
2. Formal Structure	Potential based on scenario
3. Informal Structures	Potential based on scenario
4. Rituals and Routines	Potential based on scenario
5. Symbols of power	Potential based on scenario
6. Influential Leaders	Potential based on scenario
7. Communication	Potential based on scenario
8. Key Players	Potential based on scenario
9. Control Systems	Potential based on scenario

Source: Created by author.

VBS2's combination of scripting prowess and accurate modeling can build a physically and cultural stimulating environment. With the right script, all the characteristic of the cultural cube can be replicated within a VBS2 scenario to an accurate degree to cultural training requirements and achieve training objectives.

In summation, this thesis analyzed three simulations that are categorized as cultural trainers, Tactical Iraqi, ELECT BiLAT, and VBS2.

In the first two simulations, Tactical Iraqi and ELECT BiLAT, are missing characteristics of three specific cultural themes in doctrine. Both simulations negate the process of self-awareness, cannot be trained at the collective level, and are extremely limited in their interpretation of the intangibles of culture.

When replicating the specific intangibles of culture such as the cultural cube, Tactical Iraqi and ELECT BiLAT, lack of population for cultural feedback. This lack of observable effects upon a population limits the cultural cube to text from reports or conversation from one specific leader. This single perspective of culture poorly replicates a culturally diverse environment and stifles an immerse experience.

VBS2 has the potential to be in compliance with the cultural themes in doctrine and replicate the cultural cube characteristics, but only with the proper scripting and an embedded cultural framework to ensure a replication of the cultural environment.

When the training gaps of the three simulations are compared against the characteristics a cultural competency a unit should possess, ten distinct traits are not fully developed.

The lack of self awareness training affects eight McFarland traits. Self awareness training allows one to compare one's culture to another person's culture. This comparison allows for biases to be present. If the biases are not known, then the viewing of another person's culture could be skewed without the group knowing. First, the absence of self awareness in the simulations marginalized the training the history of mainstream and nonmainstream American cultures and understand how these histories affect current society. Second, the trait of understanding the dangers of stereotyping, ethnocentrisms, and other biases and are aware of and sensitive to issues of racism and prejudice cannot be developed since self awareness training is necessary to bring out those biases.

The limitations in the intangibles of culture affect eight McFarland traits. These traits cannot be fully developed in a simulation until the intangibles of a culture are replicated in the simulation. The fist trait of specific cultural is beliefs, values, and

51

sensibilities that might affect the way they and others think or behave since beliefs, values, and sensibilities are narrow replications in the simulations. The second trait of appreciate and accept diverse beliefs, appearances, and lifestyles is hampered by limited replication of the intangibles of cultures. Last, the trait of understand that cultural differences exist and need to be accounted for in the context of military operations cannot be fully replicated with limited cultural intangibles to show the differences in culture.

Table 10. Cultural Competencies Cross Reference

16 Cultural Competencies	Self Awareness	Intangibles
Understand that culture affects their behavior and beliefs and the behavior and beliefs of others.	Cannot develop	Cannot develop
Are aware of specific cultural beliefs, values, and sensibilities that might affect the way they and others think or behave.	Cannot develop	Cannot develop
Appreciate and accept diverse beliefs, appearances, and lifestyles.		Cannot develop
Are aware that historical knowledge is constructed and, therefore, shaped by personal, political, and social forces.		
Know the history of mainstream and nonmainstream American cultures and understand how these histories affect current society.	Cannot develop	
Can understand the perspective of nonmainstream groups when learning about historical events.	Cannot develop	Cannot develop
Know about major historical events of other nations and understand how such events affect behaviors, beliefs, and relationships with others.		Cannot develop
Are aware of the similarities among groups of different cultural backgrounds and accept differences between them.	Cannot develop	Cannot develop

Understand the dangers of stereotyping, ethnocentrisms, and other biases and are aware of and sensitive to issues of racism and prejudice.	Cannot develop	
Are bilingual, multilingual, or working toward language proficiency.		
Can communicate, interact, and work positively with individuals from other cultural groups.		
Use technology to communicate with individuals and access resources from other cultures.		
Are familiar with changing cultural norms of technology (such as instant messaging, virtual workspaces, E-mail, and so on), and can interact successfully in such environments.		
Understand that cultural differences exist and need to be accounted for in the context of military operations.	Cannot develop	Cannot develop
Understand that as soldiers they are part of a widely stereotyped culture that will encounter predisposed prejudices, which will need to be overcome in cross-cultural relations.	Cannot develop	Cannot develop
Are secure and confident in their identities and capable of functioning in a way that allows others to remain secure in theirs.		

Source: Created by author.

The next chapter will discuss conclusions from this analysis and

recommendations.

CHAPTER 5

CONCLUSIONS AND RECOMMENDATIONS

Conclusions and Recommendations

> If you don't understand the cultures you are involved in; who makes the decisions in these societies; how their infrastructure is designed; the uniqueness of their values and in their taboos--you are not going to be successful.
> — George Wilson, JP 3.06, *Doctrine for Joint Urban Operations*

The above quote from Mr. George Wilson is appropriate to the forces deploying into the operational environment of today. Gen Stanley McChrystal states in his COMISAF Initial Assessment, "Afghan social, political, economic, and cultural affairs are complex and poorly understood. ISAF does not sufficiently appreciate the dynamics in local communities, nor how the insurgency, corruption, incompetent officials, power-brokers, and criminality all combine to affect the Afghan population." GEN McChrystal further states in this assessment, "A perceived lack of respect from international military troops has fueled Afghans' resentment towards the international community. International troops' apparent unwillingness to study Afghan culture and co-operate with locals, has caused mass hatred of the 'foreigners.'" Yet with all the emphasis on culture stated by Senior Army Leaders, the units with the most contact have the least amount of training.

Given the operational environment of today, the global war on terror, and our involvement in counterinsurgency wars such as Iraq and Afghanistan, the US Forces must not only change our operational strategy but redefine our training strategy as well. There is clear emphasis on the trust of the indigenous population and training of host nation forces as the keys to operational success in our security environment today. Our relevancy in the operational environment is dwindling without the development of cultural competency in tactical troops.

The task of developing cultural competency is a requirement for the US Forces to effectively dominate battle space and maintain relevancy in the operational environment today. Now the questions turn to "how does the US Army develop culture competency at the tactical level?"

Based on the analysis in chapter four, there are five conclusions that come to light. First, the US Army must have a standardized definition of culture that reflects both tangible and intangible qualities. Second, the US Army must have a standardized definition of cultural competency. Third, the US Army must define what attributes a unit should develop in order to achieve cultural competency. Fourth, cultural competency must be trained at the collective level. Last, in order to properly train the intangible aspects of culture, a framework must be developed to identify characteristics with a certain group and dynamics to compare between different groups.

The standard definition of culture would alleviate confusion and add to unity of effort in cultural diverse environments. The Peace Corps recommendation is below.

"An integrated system of learned behavior patterns that is characteristic of the members of any given society. Culture refers to the total way of life for a particular group of people. It includes what a group of people thinks, says, does and makes--its customs, language, material artifacts and shared systems of attitudes and feelings" (Peace Corps Handbook 1997, 18).

This definition of culture gives a clear emphasis to the intangibles of culture lacking in the DOD definition.

A standard definition of cultural competency will gain a common operational picture for what cultural competency looks like and strengthen unity of effort. The recommend definition of cultural competency is a "set of cultural behaviors and attitudes integrated in the practice methods of a system, agency or its professionals that enable them to work effectively in a cross-cultural situation" (Cross, Cultural Competency in Healthcare, 5).

Once the definition of cultural competency is standardized, the specific attributes a tactical unit should posses in order to be effective in a culturally diverse environment need to be defined. The cultural literate attributes of COL (Ret) Maxine McFarland set realistic characteristics of a unit to achieve the end state of culturally competency.

Cultural training must be trained at the collective level in order to be in compliance with doctrine. Although training at the individual level is necessary to build up cultural skill sets, there must be a scenario that trains unit at the collective level prior to a deployment to a CTC or theater of war in order to develop the cognitive skills to collectively look, listen, analyze and communication in the physically and cultural simulated operational environment.

Finally, a simulation has the technical ability to immerse a tactical unit into a culturally rich environment but there must be standardized model or framework to ensure the characteristics of culture are properly replicated. A recommended simulation and framework are VBS2 with multiplayer scenarios that reflect the cultural cube and cultural dynamics of a region to truly replicate the intangible aspects of a culture.

REFERENCE LIST

Books

Cross, T., B. Bazron, K. Dennis, and M. Isaacs. 1989. *Towards a culturally competent system of care*. Washington, DC: Georgetown University Child Development Center, CASSP Technical Assistance Center.

Earley, Christopher P., and Soon Ang. 2003. *Cultural intelligence individual interactions across cultures*. Chicago, IL: Stanford University Press.

Hampden-Turner, Charles and Alfons Trompennaars. 2000. *Building cross cultural competence. How to create wealth from conflicting values*. New Haven, CT: Yale University Press.

Huntington, Samuel P., and Lawrence E. Harrison, eds. 2000. *Culture matters: How values shape human progress*. New York: Basic Books.

Jasper, Melanie and Jumaa Mansour. 2004. Effective healthcare leadership. Blackwell Press.

Johnson, Gerry, and Kevan Scholes. 1997. *Exploring corporate strategy*. Saddle River, NJ: Prentice Hall

Rodriguez, B. M. 1999. *Creating inclusive and multicultural communities: Working through assumptions of culture, power, diversity and equity*. In J. Q. Adams, and J. R. Welsch, *Cultural diversity: Curriculum, classroom, & climate*. Macomb, IL: Illinois Staff and Curriculum Development Association.

Periodicals

Bonvillain, Dr. Dorothy Guy. 2006. "Cultural awareness and the WOT." *Field Artillery* (March-April): 21-27. http://.sill-www.army.mil/famag/2007/MAR_APR_2007/ Mar_Apr_07_Pages_22_27 (accessed 21 August 2009).

Connable, Ben. 2009. "All our eggs in a broken basket: How the human terrain system is undermining sustainable military cultural competence." *Military Review* (March-April): 57–64.

Jager, Sheila Miyoshi. 2007. "On the Uses of Cultural Knowledge." *Strategic Studies Institute* (November).

Mcfarland, Maxie. 2005. "Miltary Cultural Education." *Military Review* (March-April): 62–69.

Petraeus, General David H. 2006 "Learning counterinsrugency: Observations from soldiering in Iraq." *Military Review*. (October): 51.

Betancourt, Joesph R. Green, Alexander R. Carrillo, Emilo J. Park, Elyse R. 2005, "Cultural competence and health care disparities: Key perspectives and trends." *Health Affairs*: 499--505

Government Documents

Arnold, Kris A. 2006. "PMESII and the non-state actor: questioning the relevance. Research." Mongraph, School for Advance Military Studies, Leavenworth, KS.

Department of the Army. 2008. Field Manual (FM) 3-0, *Operations*. Washington, DC: Government Printing Office.

———. 2006. Field Manual (FM) 3-24 *Counterinsurgency*. Washington, DC: Government Printing Office.

Department of Health and Human Resources. 2009. HRSA strategic plan. Washington, DC: Government Printing Office.

Hall, Justin W. 2006. "T.E. Lawrence as a cultural training model for the United States Air Force." Research Report, Air Command and Staff College, Maxwell Air Force Base, Alabama

Keene, Sean T. 2007. "Know your enemy and know yourself: Assessing progress in developing cultural competence to enhance operational effectiveness." Research Project, Naval War College, Newport, RI.

U.S. Peace Corps. 1997. *Culture Matters: The Peace-Corps Cross-Cultural Handbook/Workbook*. Washington, DC: Government Printing Office.

Williams, Timothy R. 2006. "Culture--We need some of that! Cultural knowledge and army officer professional development." Research Paper, Army War College, Carlisle, PA.

Wunderle, William D. 2006. *Through the lens of cultural awareness: A primer for US armed forces deploying to Arab and Middle Eastern Countries.* Leavenworth, KS: Combat Studies Institute.

Other Sources

Anderson, R. C. (1984). Role of the reader's schema in comprehension, learning, and memory. In Learning to read in American schools: Basal readers and content texts (pp. 373-383). Laurence Earlbaum Associates.

Coles, John P. 2005 "Cultural Intelligence and joint intelligence doctrine". http://www.au.af.mil/au/awc/awcgate/ndu/jfsc_cultural_intelligence.pdf (accessed on 21 August 2009)

Davis, Alex, and Dan Fu. 2004. "Culture matters: better decision making through increased awareness." http://www.stottlerhenke.com/papers/iitsec-04-culture.pdf (accessed 15 July 2009).

Isaacs, Mareasa R., and Marva P. Benjamin. 1991 "Towards a culturally competent system of care: programs which utilize culturally competent principles: Volume II.

Martinez, Martin, and Ellen Wu. 2006. "Taking cultural competency from theory to action" http://www.cpehn.org/pdfs/Cultural%20Competency%20Brief.pdf (accessed 21 September 2009)

Official Health Resources and Services Administration Web site of the US Department of Health and Human Services. http://*www.**hrsa**.gov/*

"Overcoming biases in military problem analysis and decision-making." http://www.findarticles.com/p/articles/mi_m0IBS/is_1_28/ai_82351480 (accessed 15 July 2009).

Stafford, J. R., R. Bowman, T Ewing, J. Hanna, and A. Lopez-De Fede. 1997. *Building cultural bridges*. Bloomington, IN: National Educational Service.

Virtual Battlespace 2 website. http://virtualbattlespace.vbs2.com/ (accessed on 10 October 2009)

Texas Department of Health, National Maternal and Child Health Resource Center on Cultural Competency. 1997. Journey towards cultural competency: Lessons learned. Vienna, VA: Maternal and Children's Health Bureau Clearinghouse.